WHAT IS A
Poem?

GEOFF BARKER

Britannica®
Educational Publishing

IN ASSOCIATION WITH

ROSEN
EDUCATIONAL SERVICES

Published in 2014 by Britannica Educational Publishing (a trademark of Encyclopædia Britannica, Inc.) in association with The Rosen Publishing Group, Inc.
29 East 21st Street, New York, NY 10010

Distributed exclusively by Rosen Publishing.
To see additional Britannica Educational Publishing titles, go to rosenpublishing.com

First Edition

Britannica Educational Publishing
J.E. Luebering: Director, Core Reference Group
Anthony L. Green: Editor, Compton's by Britannica

Rosen Publishing
Hope Lourie Killcoyne: Executive Editor
Nelson Sá: Art Director

Library of Congress Cataloging-in-Publication Data

Barker, Geoff, 1963-
What is a Poem? / Geoff Barker. — First Edition.
     pages cm. — (The Britannica Common Core Library)
Includes bibliographical references and index.
ISBN 978-1-62275-220-1 (library binding) — ISBN 978-1-62275-222-5 (pbk.) — ISBN 978-1-62275-224-9 (6-pack)
1. Poetry—Juvenile literature. I. Title.
PN1031.B326 2014
808.1—dc23
                                                                                        2013022573

Manufactured in the United States of America.

CONTENTS

What Is a Poem?

A poem is a piece of writing that has rhythm, like a song. To "feel" this rhythm, it helps to read poems aloud. Poems are wonderful ways of describing how something looks, feels, or sounds, often through rhyming words.

Poems have been written for thousands of years. Poems from the Chinese *Book of Songs*, are up to 3,000 years old. Some early poems came from ancient folk songs.

Some poems might be used to describe a wonderful scene, such as a beautiful sunset over the ocean.

Other poems came from stories that were told aloud and passed down from one generation to the next.

Poems have been written in every country, from Australia to Zambia. There are poems for adults and there are also children's poems.

STORYTELLERS

Shel Silverstein wrote great poems for children. Look for his poems *Snowball*, *Sick*, or *Vegetables* in a book or on the Internet.

When you read a poem, try to read it aloud so you can hear the poem's rhythm.

Different Kinds of Poems

Poets write down words to share a feeling or idea with the reader. Poets can express their feelings or ideas by writing different kinds of poems. Narrative poems tell a story, limericks are often fun, and rhyming poems and haiku poems usually follow a specific pattern and describe nature.

Poets choose their words carefully, so each word creates just the right feeling or idea. Poets use words to tell a

Some poems are meant to excite the reader. They may end with a surprise that is completely unexpected!

message. To help make the message stay with the reader, a poet might choose to make rhymes at the end of the lines of a poem. The poet may also use a special rhythm to further share the feeling or idea of the poem. Imagine drums making the sound DUM-dum, DUM-dum, DUM-dum, DUM-dum, where the stress is on the first DUM. Poets choose words to create a beat, just like this.

Stress is when one word or sound is given special importance, so it stands out from the other words and sounds in a poem.

Themes in Poems

Poems can be about anything. They can be about the poet's feelings or about the poet's cat, dog, or home. Poets can write about a cloud, smile, ghost, peanut butter and jelly… whatever they like! Some poems are serious, while others are humorous. Themes in poems from the past have included love, journeys, and heroic battles.

Poems can be scary. Have you ever read a poem about a spooky ghost?

Poems can take different shapes. Some poems are long while others are short. Poems are written in verse. Verse is lines with the same rhythmic pattern. The verse may or may not rhyme. Just as stories are divided into paragraphs, verse can be divided into stanzas.

STORYTELLERS

Walt Whitman is one of the most famous American poets. He published his first collection of poems in 1855. Whitman is sometimes called the "father of free verse." Free verse is poetry that follows the rhythm of speech.

Poems Retold

Now that we know what poems are and why they are written, let's read and compare some wonderful poems from around the world.

It's Hard To Lose a Friend

The poet of this poem is anonymous. No one knows who wrote it.

> *It's hard to lose a friend*
> *When your heart is full of hope*
> *But it's worse to lose your towel*
> *When your eyes are full of soap.*

Compare means to look at two or more things to see how alike or different they are.

The Other Day

The writer of this poem is also unknown.

The other day
Upon the stair
I met a man
Who wasn't there.

He isn't there
Again today
Oh! How I wish
He'd go away!

Imagine losing your best friend. Could you write a poem about how that feels?

11

The Witches' Spell

This stanza is from a poem written by the English poet and playwright, William Shakespeare.

Double, double, toil and trouble;
Fire burn, and cauldron bubble.
Fillet of a fenny snake
In the cauldron boil and bake;
Eye of newt, and toe of frog,
        Wool of bat, and tongue of dog,
        Adder's fork, and blind-worm's sting,
        Lizard's leg and owlet's wing,
        For a charm of powerful trouble,
Like a hell-broth, boil and bubble.

From a Railway Carriage

This stanza is from a poem written by Scottish poet and author, Robert Louis Stevenson.

Faster than fairies, faster than witches,
Bridges and houses, hedges and ditches;
And charging along like troops in a battle,
All through the meadows the horses and cattle…

STORYTELLERS

Robert Louis Stevenson wrote many wonderful poems for children. He also wrote great novels, including *Treasure Island*.

You can "feel" the speed of the train moving faster and faster in the poem *From a Railway Carriage*.

Let's Compare

It's Hard To Lose a Friend, *The Other Day*, *The Witches' Spell*, and *From a Railway Carriage* are all narrative poems.

It's *Hard To Lose a Friend* tells the story of someone no longer having a best friend. It should be a sad poem, but the poet changes the mood in the second half, making it funny.

The Other Day tells the story of a person who thinks he or she has seen someone, but has not. It is also funny. The poet uses the same rhyme in the second and last line, so it goes round in a circle.

The witches in Shakespeare's poem use horrible ingredients to create their spell!

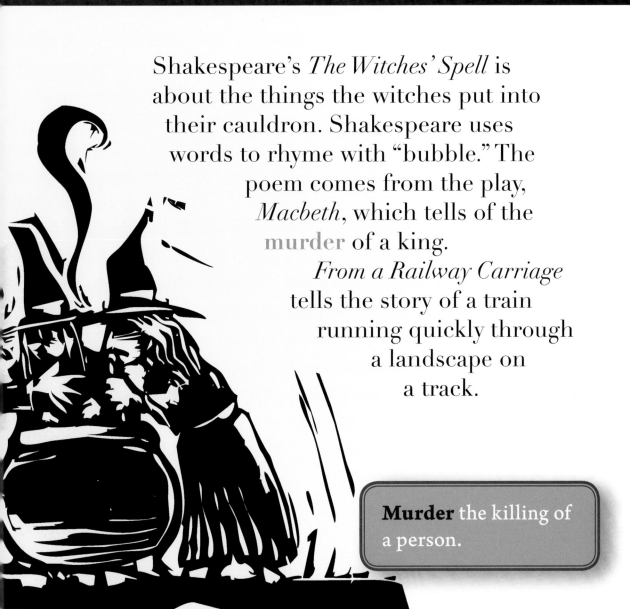

Shakespeare's *The Witches' Spell* is about the things the witches put into their cauldron. Shakespeare uses words to rhyme with "bubble." The poem comes from the play, *Macbeth*, which tells of the murder of a king.

From a Railway Carriage tells the story of a train running quickly through a landscape on a track.

Murder the killing of a person.

15

Haiku by Matsuo Basho

The first haiku poems were written more than 1,000 years ago. Haiku are three lines long. In Japanese, they have 17 syllables: five syllables in the first line, seven in the second line, and five in the last line. When Haiku are translated into English, the number of syllables can vary. Haiku have no punctuation or capital letters.

These haiku by Matsuo Basho were written more than 300 years ago. Basho is one of the most important Japanese poets.

an old pond
a frog jumps in
the splash of water

*now then, let's go out
to enjoy the snow… until
I slip and fall*

Haiku poems can be about anything, but they are often about nature.

Haiku by Natsume Soseki
These haiku were written by Natsume Soseki, a Japanese haiku writer.

over the wintry
forest, winds howl in rage
with no leaves to blow

Haiku poems may have different versions because they have been translated.

In this haiku, the subject changes. First, it is the lamp, then it becomes the stars.

the lamp once out
cool stars enter
the window frame

STORYTELLERS

Natsume Soseki was born in 1867 in Japan, and died in 1916. He also wrote novels, such as *I Am a Cat.*

Let's Compare

The four haiku poems have very different endings. The first one by Basho describes a sound in "the splash of water." We think of the quiet before, and after, the splash.

Basho's second poem is about winter. Unlike the windy scene in Soseki's poem, Basho's winter is fun. The poet could be remembering a time when he played in the snow. He realizes that he is older now, and may fall over and hurt himself.

Soseki's first poem is about a wind-blown forest in winter. The landscape is bleak and cold. Listen to the words "winds howl in rage." The winds are compared to angry animals in pain. The poem does have a surprise ending—the furious winds have "no leaves to blow."

Bleak means open to wind or weather.

The final poem by Soseki about starlight is quite magical. The poet is getting used to the dark, but it is almost as if the window frame sucks in the stars. The poem describes the moments when your eyes start getting used to the dark outside. Gradually you see more and more pinpricks of light in the night sky.

Limericks by Edward Lear

These limericks are by Edward Lear,
a famous poet from England.

There was an Old Man with a beard,
Who said, "It is just as I feared!
Two Owls and a Hen,
Four Larks and a Wren,
Have all built their nests in my beard!"

The short, funny *Old Man with a Beard* is typical of humorous limericks.

There was a Young Lady whose eyes,
Were *unique* as to color and size;
When she opened them wide,
People all turned aside,
And started away in surprise.

Unique means the only one of its kind.

More Limericks

No one knows who wrote these limericks, but they come from England and Ireland.

There was a young lady named Maggie,
Whose dog was enormous and shaggy;
The front end of him
Looked vicious and grim–
But the back end was friendly and waggy.

There once were two cats of *Kilkenny,*
Each thought that was one cat too many;
So they started to fight
And to scratch and to bite–
Now, instead of two cats, there aren't any.

People from County Kilkenny
in Ireland are often known as
"Kilkenny cats," after the poem.

Kilkenny is a
place in Ireland.

Let's Compare

The four limericks in this book have the same rhyming pattern, and they build up to a punch line at the end.

Edward Lear is famous for making limericks popular. His *Old Man with a Beard* and *Young Lady* are not real people, so he is free to be as rude as he likes about them!

The poem about the shaggy dog has a funny, surprise ending. The dog may look scary from the front, but his friendly, wagging tail tells a different story.

> **Punch line** means the final, powerful point at the end of a joke or a story.

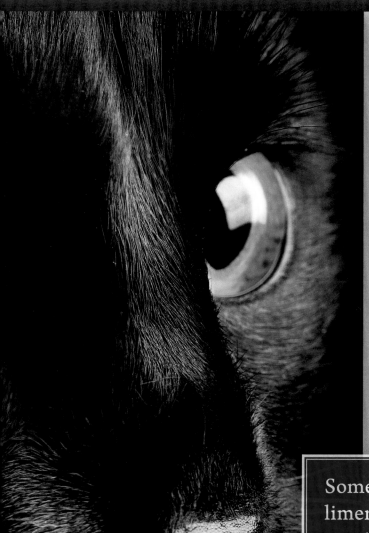

Whether the poem about the fighting cats is based on fact or fiction, it makes Kilkenny famous. People from Kilkenny also like the poem because it has become part of their history.

Some people say that the limerick about the Kilkenny cats is based on a true story.

Write Your Own Poem

Are you ready to write your own poem? Here are some steps to help you start:

1. Pick your subject: Decide what your poem is going to be about—for example, will you write about your pet, a friend, or something funny?

2. Pick a type of poem: Will a narrative poem, a haiku, or a limerick suit your poem best? Make the form of your poem match your subject.

3. Note ideas: Write down ideas that come into your mind. Combine all sorts of different words to describe what you want to say.

4. Check the rhythm: Do the words and lines sound good? Can you make them sound better?

5. Write and rewrite! Write your poem. Read it through and change anything that you do not like.

Finished? Read your poem to a friend, or one of your family members. Send it in an e-mail to your teacher or a member of your family. You could even post it onto your family's website or blog.

If you are writing a haiku, go for a walk for some inspiration. Look around you!

adder A type of snake.

anonymous Unknown or not named. It is often written as "anon." for short.

cauldron A large cooking pot.

ditches Narrow furrows or channels in the ground.

fenny snake A snake that lives in the swamps of the eastern area of England, United Kingdom.

fiction Something that is made up.

fillet A piece of meat.

folk song A simple song from a particular place.

generation People born and living at around the same time.

haiku A short poem of Japanese origin having a specific three-line structure.

humorous Funny.

ingredients The things that go into a recipe or a spell.

larks Birds.

limericks Funny types of poems with specific rhyming formulas.

meadows Fields of grass.

newt A kind of small salamander that lives mostly in water.

novels Books that tell a story.

owlet A young owl.

playwright Someone who writes plays.

poets People who write poems.

rhyming When words sound the same at the end—for example, "egg" and "leg."

rhythm A pattern of beats in music, or in words such as in a poem.

spell A magic word or recipe that is supposed to produce a particular result.

stanzas Groups of lines from a poem that go together.

starlight The light given off by the stars at night.

subject The main idea in a poem.

syllables The sounds in a word—for example, "cro-co-dile" has three syllables.

wren A type of bird.

Books

Angelou, Maya. *Poetry for Young People*. New York, NY: Sterling Children's Books, 2013.

Farrar, Sid. *The Year Comes Round: Haiku through the Seasons*. Park Ridge, IL: Albert Whitman & Company, 2012.

Kennedy, Caroline. *Poems to Learn by Heart.* New York, NY: Disney Hyperion Books, 2013.

Levin, Jonathan (ed). *Walt Whitman* (Poetry for Young People). New York, NY: Sterling Publishing, 2008.

Silverstein, Shel. *Where the Sidewalk Ends*. New York, NY: Harper Collins, 2004.

Websites

Due to the changing nature of Internet links, Rosen Publishing has developed an online list of Websites related to the subject of this book. This site is updated regularly. Please use this link to access the list:

http://www.rosenlinks.com/corel/poem

INDEX